THE LAST DANCE

SALLY MORGAN

LITTLE HARE
www.littleharebooks.com

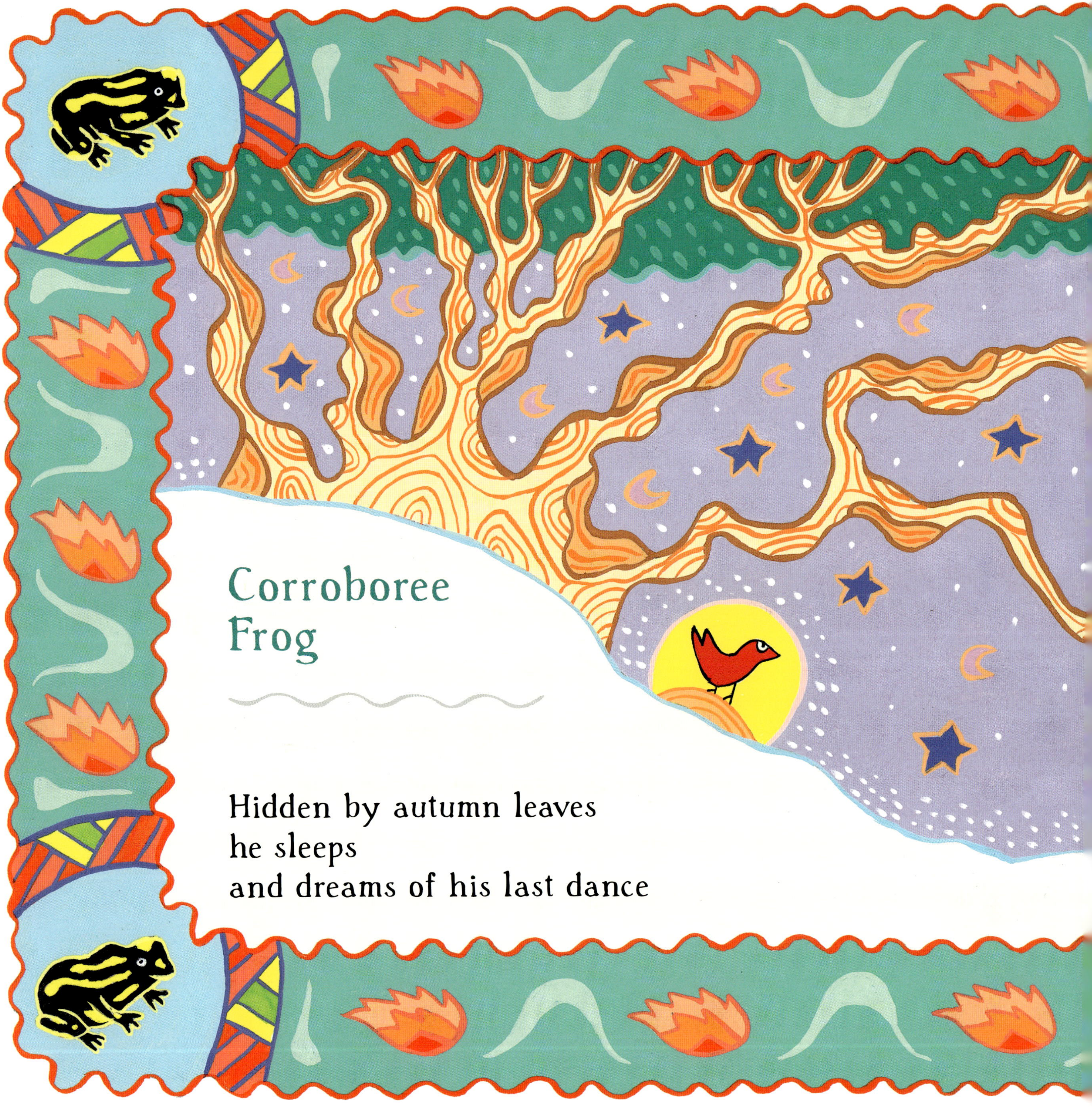

Corroboree Frog

Hidden by autumn leaves
he sleeps
and dreams of his last dance

Carnaby's Black-cockatoo

Amongst the dying trees
she hunts
for another safe home

Spotted-tailed Quoll

Beneath the moonlit sky
he shuns
the bait laid by trappers

Gilbert's Potoroo

On a windswept rock
she perches,
a wild creature with few friends

Broad-headed Snake

Over the sandstone ridge
he slides
seeking a sun-warmed shelter

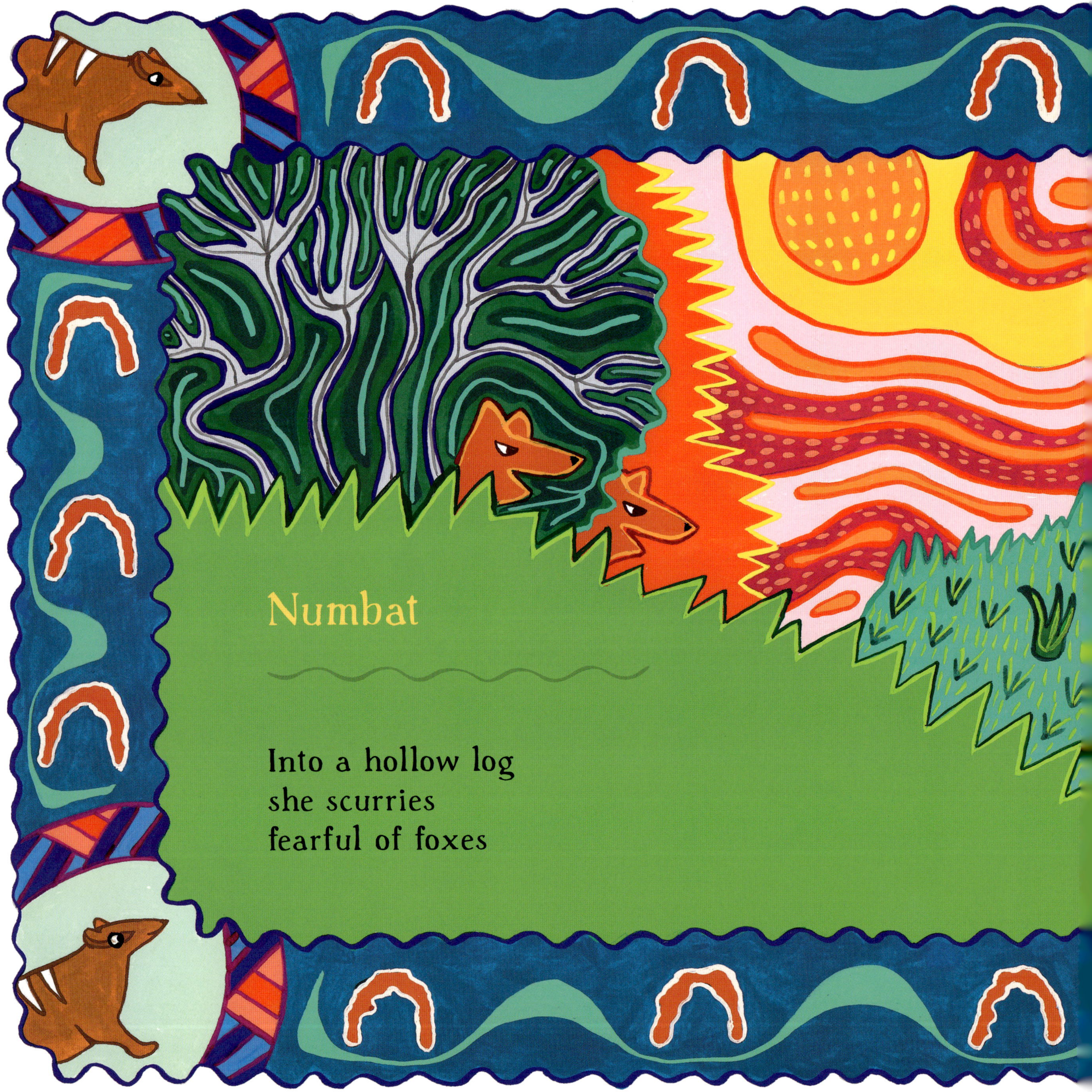

Numbat

Into a hollow log
she scurries
fearful of foxes

Flatback Turtle

Coated by slick oil
he swims
searching for clear ocean

Yellow-snouted Gecko

Across the hot earth
she races
from the blazing fire

Swift Parrot

Against the clear sky
he soars
hungry for blue-gum nectar

Dugong

Through the shallow water
she dives
escaping the fishermen

Corroboree Frog

The corroboree frog lives in the alpine region of Kosciuszko National Park, New South Wales, Australia. This tiny frog is in danger from feral animals and climate change.

Carnaby's Black-cockatoo

The Carnaby's black-cockatoo lives only in the woodlands of Western Australia. This bird struggles to find nesting places and proper food sources.

Spotted-tailed Quoll

The spotted-tailed quoll lives on the eastern coast of Australia. Its habitat is threatened and sometimes it is trapped, poisoned or shot by hunters.

Gilbert's Potoroo

The Gilbert's potoroo lives on the Mount Gardner headland of Two Peoples Bay, Western Australia. This little mammal is preyed upon by foxes and feral cats.

Broad-headed Snake

The broad-headed snake lives in sandstone areas around Sydney, New South Wales, Australia. Its rock shelters are often disturbed or damaged by humans.